Great Works Instructional Guides for **Literature**

Freckle Juice

A guide for the novel by Judy Blume
Great Works Author: Kristi Sturgeon

Publishing Credits

Corinne Burton, M.A.Ed., *President*; Emily R. Smith, M.A.Ed., *Content Director*; Lee Aucoin, *Multimedia Designer*; Stephanie Bernard, *Assistant Editor*; Don Tran, *Production Artist*; Amber Goff, *Editorial Assistant*

Image Credits

iStock (cover; pages 1, 12); Shutterstock (pages 11, 21, 27, 30, 50)

Standards

© 2007 Teachers of English to Speakers of Other Languages, Inc. (TESOL)
© 2007 Board of Regents of the University of Wisconsin System. World-Class Instructional Design and Assessment (WIDA)
© Copyright 2010. National Governors Association Center for Best Practices and Council of Chief State School Officers. All rights reserved.

Shell Education

5301 Oceanus Drive
Huntington Beach, CA 92649-1030
http://www.shelleducation.com
ISBN 978-1-4807-6993-9
© 2015 Shell Educational Publishing, Inc.
Printed in USA. WOR004

Table of Contents

How to Use This Literature Guide 4
   Theme Thoughts 4
   Vocabulary 5
   Analyzing the Literature 6
   Reader Response 6
   Guided Close Reading 6
   Making Connections 7
   Language Learning 7
   Story Elements 7
   Culminating Activity 8
   Comprehension Assessment 8
   Response to Literature 8

Correlation to the Standards 8
   Purpose and Intent of Standards 8
   How to Find Standards Correlations 8
   Standards Correlation Chart 9
   TESOL and WIDA Standards 10

About the Author—Judy Blume 11
   Possible Texts for Text Comparisons 11

Book Summary of *Freckle Juice* 12
   Cross-Curricular Connection 12
   Possible Texts for Text Sets 12

Teacher Plans and Student Pages 13
   Pre-Reading Theme Thoughts 13
   Section 1: Chapter 1 14
   Section 2: Chapter 2 24
   Section 3: Chapter 3 34
   Section 4: Chapter 4 43
   Section 5: Chapter 5 52

Post-Reading Activities 61
   Post-Reading Theme Thoughts 61
   Culminating Activity: We Are All Different 62
   Comprehension Assessment 66
   Response to Literature: We All Make Mistakes 68

Answer Key 71

How to Use This Literature Guide

Today's standards demand rigor and relevance in the reading of complex texts. The units in this series guide teachers in a rich and deep exploration of worthwhile works of literature for classroom study. The most rigorous instruction can also be interesting and engaging!

Many current strategies for effective literacy instruction have been incorporated into these instructional guides for literature. Throughout the units, text-dependent questions are used to determine comprehension of the book as well as student interpretation of the vocabulary words. The books chosen for the series are complex and are exemplars of carefully crafted works of literature. Close reading is used throughout the units to guide students toward revisiting the text and using textual evidence to respond to prompts orally and in writing. Students must analyze the story elements in multiple assignments for each section of the book. All of these strategies work together to rigorously guide students through their study of literature.

The next few pages describe how to use this guide for a purposeful and meaningful literature study. Each section of this guide is set up in the same way to make it easier for you to implement the instruction in your classroom.

Theme Thoughts

The great works of literature used throughout this series have important themes that have been relevant to people for many years. Many of the themes will be discussed during the various sections of this instructional guide. However, it would also benefit students to have independent time to think about the key themes of the book.

Before students begin reading, have them complete the *Pre-Reading Theme Thoughts* (page 13). This graphic organizer will allow students to think about the themes outside the context of the story. They'll have the opportunity to evaluate statements based on important themes and defend their opinions. Be sure to keep students' papers for comparison to the *Post-Reading Theme Thoughts* (page 61). This graphic organizer is similar to the pre-reading activity. However, this time, students will be answering the questions from the point of view of one of the characters in the book. They have to think about how the character would feel about each statement and defend their thoughts. To conclude the activity, have students compare what they thought about the themes before they read the book to what the characters discovered during the story.

How to Use This Literature Guide (cont.)

Vocabulary

Each teacher reference vocabulary overview page has definitions and sentences about how key vocabulary words are used in the section. These words should be introduced and discussed with students. Students will use these words in different activities throughout the book.

On some of the vocabulary student pages, students are asked to answer text-related questions about vocabulary words from the sections. The following question stems will help you create your own vocabulary questions if you'd like to extend the discussion.

- How does this word describe _____'s character?
- How does this word connect to the problem in this story?
- How does this word help you understand the setting?
- Tell me how this word connects to the main idea of this story.
- What visual pictures does this word bring to your mind?
- Why do you think the author used this word?

At times, you may find that more work with the words will help students understand their meanings and importance. These quick vocabulary activities are a good way to further study the words.

- Students can play vocabulary concentration. Make one set of cards that has the words on them and another set with the definitions. Then, have students lay them out on the table and play concentration. The goal of the game is to match vocabulary words with their definitions. For early readers or English language learners, the two sets of cards could be the words and pictures of the words.

- Students can create word journal entries about the words. Students choose words they think are important and then describe why they think each word is important within the book. Early readers or English language learners could instead draw pictures about the words in a journal.

- Students can create puppets and use them to act out the vocabulary words from the stories. Students may also enjoy telling their own character-driven stories using vocabulary words from the original stories.

How to Use This Literature Guide (cont.)

Analyzing the Literature

After you have read each section with students, hold a small-group or whole-class discussion. Provided on the teacher reference page for each section are leveled questions. The questions are written at two levels of complexity to allow you to decide which questions best meet the needs of your students. The Level 1 questions are typically less abstract than the Level 2 questions. These questions are focused on the various story elements, such as character, setting, and plot. Be sure to add further questions as your students discuss what they've read. For each question, a few key points are provided for your reference as you discuss the book with students.

Reader Response

In today's classrooms, there are often great readers who are below average writers. So much time and energy is spent in classrooms getting students to read on grade level that little time is left to focus on writing skills. To help teachers include more writing in their daily literacy instruction, each section of this guide has a literature-based reader response prompt. Each of the three genres of writing is used in the reader responses within this guide: narrative, informative/explanatory, and opinion. Before students write, you may want to allow them time to draw pictures related to the topic.

Guided Close Reading

Within each section of this guide, it is suggested that you closely reread a portion of the text with your students. Page numbers are given, but since some versions of the books may have different page numbers, the sections to be reread are described by location as well. After rereading the section, there are a few text-dependent questions to be answered by students.

Working space has been provided to help students prepare for the group discussion. They should record their thoughts and ideas on the activity page and refer to it during your discussion. Rather than just taking notes, you may want to require students to write complete responses to the questions before discussing them with you.

Encourage students to read one question at a time and then go back to the text and discover the answer. Work with students to ensure that they use the text to determine their answers rather than making unsupported inferences. Suggested answers are provided in the answer key.

How to Use This Literature Guide (cont.)

Guided Close Reading (cont.)

The generic open-ended stems below can be used to write your own text-dependent questions if you would like to give students more practice.

- What words in the story support . . . ?
- What text helps you understand . . . ?
- Use the book to tell why _____ happens.
- Based on the events in the story, . . . ?
- Show me the part in the text that supports . . . .
- Use the text to tell why . . . .

Making Connections

The activities in this section help students make cross-curricular connections to mathematics, science, social studies, fine arts, or other curricular areas. These activities require higher-order thinking skills from students but also allow for creative thinking.

Language Learning

A special section has been set aside to connect the literature to language conventions. Through these activities, students will have opportunities to practice the conventions of standard English grammar, usage, capitalization, and punctuation.

Story Elements

It is important to spend time discussing what the common story elements are in literature. Understanding the characters, setting, plot, and theme can increase students' comprehension and appreciation of the story. If teachers begin discussing these elements in early childhood, students will more likely internalize the concepts and look for the elements in their independent reading. Another very important reason for focusing on the story elements is that students will be better writers if they think about how the stories they read are constructed.

In the story elements activities, students are asked to create work related to the characters, setting, or plot. Consider having students complete only one of these activities. If you give students a choice on this assignment, each student can decide to complete the activity that most appeals to him or her. Different intelligences are used so that the activities are diverse and interesting to all students.

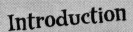
How to Use This Literature Guide (cont.)

Culminating Activity

At the end of this instructional guide is a creative culminating activity that allows students the opportunity to share what they've learned from reading the book. This activity is open ended so that students can push themselves to create their own great works within your language arts classroom.

Comprehension Assessment

The questions in this section require students to think about the book they've read as well as the words that were used in the book. Some questions are tied to quotations from the book to engage students and require them to think about the text as they answer the questions.

Response to Literature

Finally, students are asked to respond to the literature by drawing pictures and writing about the characters and stories. A suggested rubric is provided for teacher reference.

Correlation to the Standards

Shell Education is committed to producing educational materials that are research and standards based. As part of this effort, we have correlated all of our products to the academic standards of all 50 states, the District of Columbia, the Department of Defense Dependents Schools, and all Canadian provinces.

Purpose and Intent of Standards

Standards are designed to focus instruction and guide adoption of curricula. Standards are statements that describe the criteria necessary for students to meet specific academic goals. They define the knowledge, skills, and content students should acquire at each level. Standards are also used to develop standardized tests to evaluate students' academic progress. Teachers are required to demonstrate how their lessons meet standards. Standards are used in the development of all of our products, so educators can be assured they meet high academic standards.

How to Find Standards Correlations

To print a customized correlation report of this product for your state, visit our website at http://www.shelleducation.com and follow the online directions. If you require assistance in printing correlation reports, please contact our Customer Service Department at 1-877-777-3450.

Correlation to the Standards (cont.)

Standards Correlation Chart

The lessons in this book were written to support today's college and career readiness standards. The following chart indicates which lessons address each standard.

College and Career Readiness Standard	Section
Read closely to determine what the text says explicitly and to make logical inferences from it; cite specific textual evidence when writing or speaking to support conclusions drawn from the text. (R.1)	Guided Close Reading Sections 1–5; Vocabulary Activity Sections 2–4; Making Connections Section 5; Post-Reading Response to Literature
Determine central ideas or themes of a text and analyze their development; summarize the key supporting details and ideas. (R.2)	Analyzing the Literature Sections 1–5; Guided Close Reading Sections 1–5; Post-Reading Theme Thoughts; Culminating Activity
Analyze how and why individuals, events, or ideas develop and interact over the course of a text. (R.3)	Analyzing the Literature Sections 1–5; Making Connections Section 5; Story Elements Section 5; Post-Reading Theme Thoughts; Culminating Activity; Post-Reading Response to Literature
Interpret words and phrases as they are used in a text, including determining technical, connotative, and figurative meanings, and analyze how specific word choices shape meaning or tone. (R.4)	Guided Close Reading Sections 1–5; Vocabulary Activity Section 4
Analyze the structure of texts, including how specific sentences, paragraphs, and larger portions of the text (e.g., a section, chapter, scene, or stanza) relate to each other and the whole. (R.5)	Guided Close Reading Sections 1–5; Vocabulary Activity Section 3
Read and comprehend complex literary and informational texts independently and proficiently. (R.10)	Guided Close Reading Sections 1–5
Write arguments to support claims in an analysis of substantive topics or texts using valid reasoning and relevant and sufficient evidence. (W.1)	Reader Response Sections 1, 4; Guided Close Reading Sections 1–5; Making Connections Sections 2, 4; Story Elements Sections 1–5; Making Connections Section 5; Post-Reading Theme Thoughts; Culminating Activity; Post-Reading Response to Literature
Write informative/explanatory texts to examine and convey complex ideas and information clearly and accurately through the effective selection, organization, and analysis of content. (W.2)	Reader Response Section 1
Write narratives to develop real or imagined experiences or events using effective technique, well-chosen details and well-structured event sequences. (W.3)	Reader Response Sections 2–3, 5; Story Elements Sections 2–3
Produce clear and coherent writing in which the development, organization, and style are appropriate to task, purpose, and audience. (W.4)	Guided Close Reading Sections 1–5; Story Elements Sections 1–5; Making Connections Sections 2, 4; Post-Reading Theme Thoughts; Culminating Activity; Post-Reading Response to Literature

Standards Correlation Chart (cont.)

College and Career Readiness Standard	Section
Demonstrate command of the conventions of standard English grammar and usage when writing or speaking. (L.1)	Guided Close Reading Sections 1–5; Vocabulary Activity Section 5; Story Elements Sections 1–5; Making Connections Sections 2, 4; Post-Reading Theme Thoughts; Culminating Activity; Post-Reading Response to Literature
Demonstrate command of the conventions of standard English capitalization, punctuation, and spelling when writing. (L.2)	Guided Close Reading Sections 1–5; Vocabulary Activity Section 5; Story Elements Sections 1–5; Making Connections Sections 2, 4; Language Learning Sections 1–5; Post-Reading Theme Thoughts; Culminating Activity; Post-Reading Response to Literature
Apply knowledge of language to understand how language functions in different contexts, to make effective choices for meaning or style, and to comprehend more fully when reading or listening. (L.3)	Analyzing the Literature Sections 1–5; Guided Close Reading Sections 1–5; Vocabulary Section 4
Determine or clarify the meaning of unknown and multiple-meaning words and phrases by using context clues, analyzing meaningful word parts, and consulting general and specialized reference materials, as appropriate. (L.4)	Vocabulary Sections 1–5
Demonstrate understanding of figurative language, word relationships, and nuances in word meanings. (L.5)	Vocabulary Section 5
Acquire and use accurately a range of general academic and domain-specific words and phrases sufficient for reading, writing, speaking, and listening at the college and career readiness level; demonstrate independence in gathering vocabulary knowledge when encountering an unknown term important to comprehension or expression. (L.6)	Vocabulary Sections 1–5; Analyzing the Literature Sections 1–5; Guided Close Reading Sections 1–5; Post-Reading Theme Thoughts; Culminating Activity; Post Reading Response to Literature

TESOL and WIDA Standards

The lessons in this book promote English language development for English language learners. The following TESOL and WIDA English Language Development Standards are addressed through the activities in this book:

- **Standard 1:** English language learners communicate for social and instructional purposes within the school setting.

- **Standard 2:** English language learners communicate information, ideas and concepts necessary for academic success in the content area of language arts.

About the Author—Judy Blume

Judy Blume was born on February 12, 1938, in New Jersey. As a child, she had a very active imagination. Blume loved to make up stories in her head, but she never wrote them down. As an adult, she still had the urge to tell stories, but it wasn't until her children were in preschool that she began writing. Many of her books are set in New Jersey, where she spent her childhood. In 1961, Blume earned a bachelor of science degree in education from New York University. She later spent time in New Mexico, Connecticut, and Maine, which became the settings of some of her other works. She believes she has to truly know a place before committing to it as a book setting.

Blume currently resides in the eastern United States with her husband, George Cooper, a nonfiction writer. Blume has won more than 90 literary awards, including three lifetime achievement awards. She is the founder and trustee of The Kids Fund, a charitable and educational foundation. She is also involved with The Authors Guild, the Society of Children's Book Writers and Illustrators, the Key West Literary Seminar, and the National Coalition Against Censorship.

Blume's works have been featured on *The New York Times* Best Seller's list, have been translated into 32 languages, and have sold over 82 million copies. You can learn more about Judy Blume and her books on her website: **http://www.judyblume.com**.

Possible Texts for Text Comparisons

Blume has written two other books in the picture and storybook category: *The Pain and the Great One* and *The One in the Middle Is the Green Kangaroo*. Either book would make for nice comparisons to *Freckle Juice* for young readers.

Book Summary of *Freckle Juice*

Andrew wishes he had freckles like his classmate, Nicky Lane. He thinks that if he had freckles, his mother wouldn't be able to tell if his neck and face were dirty and he wouldn't have to wash them.

Andrew finally gets the nerve to ask Nicky how he got all his freckles. Another classmate, Sharon, overhears and decides to offer a secret recipe to Andrew. She charges him fifty cents for her "freckle juice" recipe.

Andrew mixes up the concoction of grape juice, vinegar, mustard, and other smelly ingredients at home and waits for the magic to happen, but all it does is make him feel sick to his stomach. He stays home from school the next day. When he returns to school, he doesn't want to give Sharon the satisfaction of knowing that her recipe didn't work, so instead he uses a blue magic marker to draw freckles all over his face. Everyone in class laughs at Andrew's blue freckles, but his teacher gives him her "secret formula" for removing freckles.

When Andrew returns to class with a freckle-free face, Nicky Lane asks for the recipe for freckle remover, admitting that he hates his freckles. Sharon overhears the conversation and tells Nicky that she has a recipe that can get rid of freckles. Before Andrew can say anything to warn Nicky, Sharon makes a super-duper frog face at him.

Cross-Curricular Connection

This book can be used in a science unit on mixtures and solutions, as well as a unit on biology and genetics.

Possible Texts for Text Sets

- Catling, Patrick Skene. *The Chocolate Touch*. HarperCollins, 2006.
- Cleary, Beverly. *Ramona the Brave*. Avon Camelot, 2013.
- DeClements, Barthe. *Nothing's Fair in Fifth Grade*. Puffin, 2008.
- Rockwell, Thomas. *How to Eat Fried Worms*. Yearling, 2006.
- Smith, Robert Kimmel. *Chocolate Fever*. Puffin, 2006.

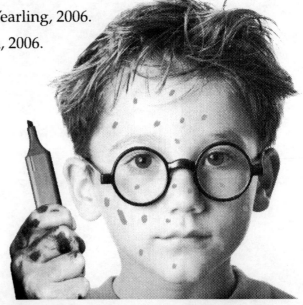

Pre-Reading Theme Thoughts

Directions: Draw a picture of a happy face or a sad face. Your face should show how you feel about each statement. Then, use words to say what you think about each statement.

Statement	How Do You Feel? 😊 😞	Explain Your Answer
Everyone can be trusted.		
Most people want to change something about themselves.		
Being the center of attention is fun.		
Teachers help build confidence in students.		

Vocabulary Overview

Key words and phrases from this section are provided below with definitions and sentences about how the words are used in the story. Introduce and discuss these important vocabulary words with students. If you think these words or other words in the story warrant more time devoted to them, there are suggestions in the introduction for other vocabulary activities (page 5).

Word	Definition	Sentence about Text
freckle	a small, brownish spot on the skin	Andrew wants **freckles** like Nicky's.
million	a cardinal number; a thousand times a thousand; 1,000,000	Nicky Lane has about a **million** freckles.
wart	a small, often hard, abnormal elevation on the skin	Andrew has two **warts** on his finger.
plenty	a full or abundant supply or amount	Andrew has **plenty** of time to count Nicky's freckles.
giggle	to laugh in a silly way, usually high pitched with short, repeated gasps	The reading group **giggles** as Andrew hurries to get ready.
poked	prodded or pushed, especially with something narrow or pointed, such as a finger or stick	After the bell rings, Andrew **pokes** Nicky on the shoulder.
recipe	a set of instructions for making or preparing something, usually a food dish	Sharon wants to sell the freckle juice **recipe** to Andrew.
mouthful	the amount a mouth can hold	Andrew wonders if Sharon ever gets a **mouthful** of bugs when she opens her mouth.
wiggle	to move with short, quick, irregular movements	Sharon often **wiggles** her tongue around her mouth.
inspect	to look carefully at something; to examine	Andrew **inspects** Sharon's face for freckles.

Vocabulary Activity

Directions: Choose at least two words from the story. Draw a picture that shows what these words mean. Label your picture.

Words from the Story

freckle	million	wart	plenty	inspect
giggle	poked	recipe	mouthful	wiggle

Directions: Answer this question.

1. What kind of **recipe** does Sharon want to sell to Andrew?

_____

Analyzing the Literature

Provided below are discussion questions you can use in small groups, with the whole class, or for written assignments. Each question is written at two levels so that you can choose the right question for each group of students. For each question, a few key points are provided for your reference as you discuss the book with students.

Story Element	Level 1	Level 2	Key Discussion Points
Character	What is special about Nicky Lane?	Why does Andrew want freckles like Nicky Lane's?	Nicky Lane has a million freckles. Andrew wants freckles like Nicky's because he thinks his mother would never know if his neck was dirty. Andrew would not have to wash, and he would never be late for school.
Plot	Why does Andrew's reading group giggle at him?	Who in his reading group especially bothers Andrew and why?	His reading group giggles because Andrew isn't paying attention and isn't prepared when Miss Kelly calls on him to read. Sharon especially bothers Andrew because she thinks she knows everything.
Setting	How does Andrew feel about being line leader?	What frustrates Andrew about being a line leader?	They are both in line and are line leaders. They are getting ready to go home. Andrew is glad that he finally gets to be line leader, but it annoys him that it is at the same time as Sharon.
Plot	What makes Andrew doubt that the freckle juice will work?	Why is Andrew skeptical of Sharon's recipe?	She charges Andrew 50 cents for the freckle juice recipe. Andrew doesn't believe Sharon because he has never heard of freckle juice before.
Character	Why does Sharon's tongue remind Andrew of a frog catching flies?	Why is Andrew inspecting Sharon's face?	Sharon always opens her mouth and wiggles her tongue around, making Andrew think of a frog. He is inspecting Sharon's face because he is looking for freckles.

Reader Response

Think

Think about your own appearance. Do you have freckles? If so, do you like them? If not, how do you feel about them?

Opinion Writing Prompt

Explain whether or not you would like to have freckles. If you already have freckles, how do you feel about them?

_____

_____

_____

_____

_____

_____

_____

_____

_____

_____

_____

_____

_____

Name _____ Date _____

Guided Close Reading

Closely reread the section that starts with, "I was wondering about your freckles . . . ." Continue until, "Who asked *you*?"

Directions: Think about these questions. In the space below, write ideas as you think about the answers. Be ready to share your answers.

❶ What words in the passage support the idea that Nicky is annoyed with Andrew?

❷ Use the book to tell why Andrew responds to his teacher with the thought, "Some luck!"

❸ In what way does Andrew continue to show that Sharon annoys him?

Making Connections–Make a Million

Andrew claims Nicky Lane has about a million freckles. They are all over his face, ears, and the back of his neck.

Directions: Think of six different ways to make the number one million (for example: 3,000,000 – 2,000,000 = 1,000,000). Write one number sentence using each operation. Then, write two more of your choice.

addition	
subtraction	
multiplication	
division	

Language Learning-Punctuation

Directions: Decide if the following sentences are written with the correct punctuation. Write the word *correct* if no corrections need to be made. If needed, write the word *incorrect* and rewrite the sentence with the necessary corrections.

Language Hints!

- Quotation marks are used for dialogue.
- Begin sentences with capital letters.

Sentence	Correct/Incorrect	Rewritten Sentence
1. Miss Kelly called, Andrew, are you paying attention?		
2. "what do you want?" Nicky asked.		
3. "Do you want to know how to get them?" Sharon asked.		
4. "It will cost you fifty cents," Sharon whispered.		
5. Sharon said, I've got six on my nose.		

Story Elements-Character

Directions: Andrew asks Nicky Lane how he got his freckles. Rewrite this scene from Nicky's point of view.

_____

_____

_____

_____

_____

_____

_____

_____

_____

_____

_____

_____

_____

Name _____ Date _____

Story Elements-Setting

Directions: Andrew mentions that he sits behind Nicky Lane. Make your ideal seating chart of the students in your class. You can place students wherever you want in your classroom!

Story Elements-Plot

Directions: Make a prediction! What do you think is in Sharon's secret freckle juice recipe? Include the ingredients and directions you think it takes to make the secret recipe.

Sharon's Freckle Juice Recipe

Ingredients

_____

_____

_____

_____

Directions

_____

_____

_____

_____

_____

Vocabulary Overview

Key words and phrases from this section are provided below with definitions and sentences about how the words are used in the story. Introduce and discuss these important vocabulary words with students. If you think these words or other words in the story warrant more time devoted to them, there are suggestions in the introduction for other vocabulary activities (page 5).

Word	Definition	Sentence about Text
secret	something kept hidden from others; known only by a few people	Sharon has a **secret** recipe for Andrew.
allowance	a sum of money set aside for a particular purpose	Fifty cents is five weeks of Andrew's **allowance**.
combination	the series of numbers used to set or unset a lock	Andrew needs a **combination** to open his safe-bank.
wrapped	enclosed something	Andrew **wraps** his dimes in a tissue.
bathrobe	a long, loose, coat-like garment that is often tied with a belt	Mrs. Marcus hurries over to Andrew in her **bathrobe.**
begged	asked in a very serious and emotional way	Andrew **begs** his mom to skip the neck and face washing.
patted	tapped lightly or gently	Sharon **pats** her pocket where the recipe is hidden.
arithmetic	the method of computation; the most basic part of mathematics	The class works on **arithmetic** first thing in the morning.
aimed	positioned or directed	Andrew **aims** the folded tissue at Sharon.
aisle	a walkway between seats	The recipe lands in the middle of the **aisle.**

Vocabulary Activity

Directions: Draw lines to match the sentences.

Sentence Beginnings

Mrs. Marcus almost trips

It is five weeks

He **wraps** them in a tissue

Andrew turns the **combination**

The recipe lands in the

Sentence Endings

and stuffs them in his pocket.

of his safe-bank to the right numbers.

middle of the **aisle**.

of Andrew's **allowance**.

on her long **bathrobe**.

Directions: Answer this question.

1. What lands in the middle of the **aisle** and what happens to Andrew?

_____

_____

Analyzing the Literature

Provided below are discussion questions you can use in small groups, with the whole class, or for written assignments. Each question is written at two levels so that you can choose the right question for each group of students. For each question, a few key points are provided for your reference as you discuss the book with students.

Story Element	Level 1	Level 2	Key Discussion Points
Plot	What is Andrew thinking about while he tries to go to sleep?	Why does Andrew think nobody in his family has freckles?	Andrew has trouble sleeping because he keeps thinking about the freckle juice. He thinks his family must not have freckles because no one knows the freckle juice recipe.
Character	Andrew doesn't like the idea of paying Sharon. What is his plan if the recipe does not work?	How do you know that 50 cents is a lot of money to Andrew?	It takes Andrew five weeks of saving his allowance for the 50 cents. Andrew plans on asking for his money back if the recipe does not work.
Character	Describe Andrew's morning.	What does Andrew beg of his mother?	Andrew's mother is in her bathrobe with curlers in her hair. Andrew begs his mother to skip washing his ears and neck since he is in a hurry.
Setting	Where do Andrew and Sharon sit in relation to each other?	How does the aisle cause a problem for Andrew?	Andrew and Sharon sit next to each other with an aisle in between them. The aisle allows too much space and the recipe falls to the floor causing Andrew to fall when he tries to reach it.
Plot	Who are the only two people to not laugh when Andrew falls?	Why doesn't Miss Kelly laugh when Andrew falls?	Andrew and Miss Kelly are the only people who do not laugh when he falls. Miss Kelly doesn't laugh because she is disappointed that Andrew is not paying attention and playing around in class again.

Name _____ Date _____

Reader Response

Think

Andrew keeps his money in a safe-bank that requires a combination to open. Think about what you keep safe and why.

Narrative Writing Prompt

Write about something that you keep safe. Explain why you keep it safe and why it is important to you.

_____

_____

_____

_____

_____

_____

_____

_____

Name _____ Date _____

Guided Close Reading

Closely reread the section starting with, "Sharon was already at her desk . . . ." Stop with, ". . . Sharon opened a book and pretended to read."

Directions: Think about these questions. In the space below, write ideas as you think about the answers. Be ready to share your answers.

❶ What evidence supports the idea that Sharon is trying to make Andrew mad?

❷ What text shows Andrew trying to bother Sharon back and make her mad?

❸ Based on the events in the story, why doesn't Sharon show the recipe first?

Making Connections–Making a Change

Andrew insists that he wants freckles all over. He is determined to make it happen. What would you want to change about yourself?

Directions: Think of something you would change if you could. What would it be and why? Draw a picture of yourself with the new look. Write reasons why you would want the new look.

_____

_____

_____

_____

Name _____ Date _____

Making Connections–Money Math

Directions: The freckle juice recipe costs 50 cents. Andrew grabs five dimes and brings them to school. He also could have used two quarters or 10 nickels. What other ways are there to make 50 cents? Think of six other combinations that each add up to 50 cents.

1.

2.

3.

4.

5.

6.

Language Learning–Awesome Adjectives

Directions: Think of five adjectives for each of the three characters in the bubbles. How would you describe these characters so far?

Language Hints!

- An adjective is a word that describes a noun.

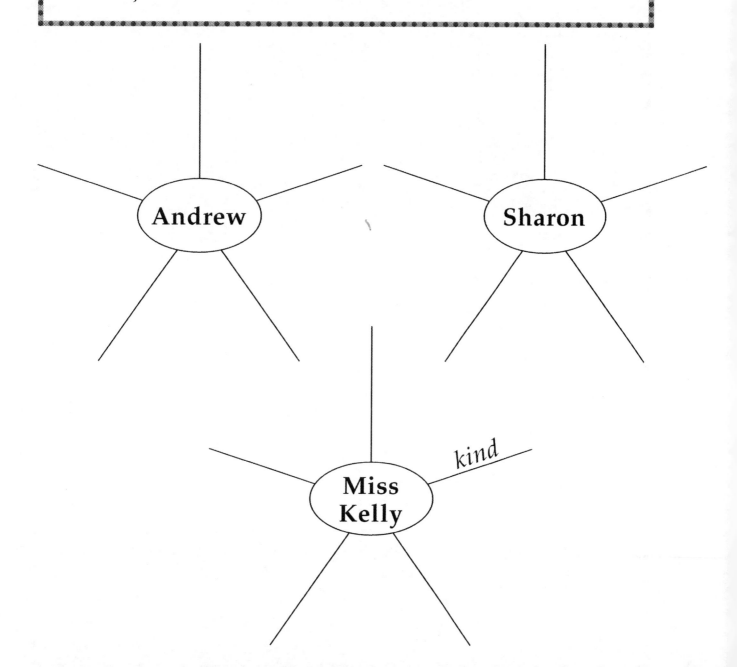

Andrew

Sharon

Miss
Kelly

kind

Name _____ Date _____

Story Elements–Setting

Directions: Andrew races to school, excited to get the recipe from Sharon. He probably wants to take the fastest route to school. Design a map with Andrew's house and his school on it. Show which way he goes to get there quickly.

Story Elements–Character

Directions: Andrew has now been laughed at twice by his classmates. Write a journal entry as if you were Andrew. How do you feel after getting laughed at? Would you have done anything differently? Why or why not?

_____

_____

_____

_____

_____

_____

_____

_____

_____

_____

_____

_____

Vocabulary Overview

Key words and phrases from this section are provided below with definitions and sentences about how the words are used in the story. Introduce and discuss these important vocabulary words with students. If you think these words or other words in the story warrant more time devoted to them, there are suggestions in the introduction for other vocabulary activities (page 5).

Word	Definition	Sentence about Text
sweaty	covered with sweat	Andrew thinks his foot might get too **sweaty**.
blur	to obscure by smearing	Andrew doesn't want the ink to **blur** on the recipe, so he doesn't put it inside his sock.
panted	breathed hard and quickly	Andrew **pants** as he runs up to the door.
dealing	passing out or distributing	His mother is **dealing** cards when he gets there.
dashed	rushed or hurried	Andrew **dashes** home to read the recipe.
average	a typical amount	Sharon claims that one glass of freckle juice makes an **average** amount of freckles.
speck	a small amount; little bit; particle	The recipe calls for a **speck** of onion.
basement	an area or part of a building that is underground	Mrs. Marcus keeps onions in the **basement.**
tilted	leaned, inclined, sloped, or slanted	Andrew **tilts** his head back to drink the freckle juice.
gulped	swallowed eagerly	Andrew **gulps** down the awful tasting freckle juice.

Vocabulary Activity

Directions: Each of these sentences contains a word from the story. Cut apart these sentence strips. Put the sentences in order based on the events in the story.

Andrew gets an onion from the **basement**.

Andrew **dashes** home to read the recipe.

Andrew **gulps** down the awful tasting freckle juice.

Andrew's foot might get too **sweaty**, so he doesn't put the recipe inside his sock.

Andrew's mother is **dealing** cards when he gets there.

Analyzing the Literature

Provided below are discussion questions you can use in small groups, with the whole class, or for written assignments. Each question is written at two levels so that you can choose the right question for each group of students. For each question, a few key points are provided for your reference as you discuss the book with students.

Story Element	Level 1	Level 2	Key Discussion Points
Plot	Where does Andrew put the secret recipe on his way home?	Why does Andrew worry about where to put the recipe on his way home?	Andrew puts the recipe in his shoe. He does not put it inside his sock because he thinks it will be too sweaty and it might blur the ink.
Character	What is Andrew's mom doing when he arrives at Mrs. Marcus's house for the key?	Why does Andrew's mom remind him to use his manners?	Mrs. Marcus is dealing cards when he gets there. She reminds Andrew to use his manners because he does not say hello to the other ladies.
Plot	How long does Andrew have to make the juice before his mom gets home?	Why does Andrew hope there is no cooking required in the recipe?	Andrew has one hour before his mom gets home. Andrew hopes there is no cooking required because he is not allowed to turn on the oven or stove.
Plot	How does Andrew try to make the recipe taste better?	How does Andrew feel as he's about to drink the freckle juice?	Andrew adds an ice cube because most drinks taste better cold. Andrew holds his nose because it eliminates the ability to taste if you cannot smell.

Reader Response

Think

Andrew attempts to make freckle juice all by himself. Think about a recipe that you have made all by yourself.

Narrative Writing Prompt

Write about something you have made all by yourself. What ingredients did you need? Was it easy? Were you successful? How did it taste?

_____

_____

_____

_____

_____

_____

_____

_____

_____

Guided Close Reading

Closely reread the beginning of the chapter. Stop at, "... he'd gotten better since last fall."

Directions: Think about these questions. In the space below, write ideas as you think about the answers. Be ready to share your answers.

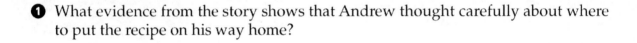

❶ What evidence from the story shows that Andrew thought carefully about where to put the recipe on his way home?

❷ Based on the events in the story, why do you think Andrew decides to wait to read the recipe until he gets home?

❸ What part in the story proves Andrew forgets that he has to pick up the house key from his mom?

Making Connections-Collecting Data

Directions: Complete the chart by tallying how many students have or do not have freckles in your class. Mark one tally mark for each student in the appropriate box. Then, count the total numbers of students with freckles and with no freckles and record that data.

Attribute	Number of Students	Total
Freckles		
No Freckles		

Directions: Create a math problem using the totals. Give the problem to a friend to solve.

Name _____ Date _____

Language Learning–Make It Plural

Directions: Read the singular noun in the first column. Think about what rule it follows to make it plural (add –s, add –es, or irregular). Write the rule and correct plural spelling in the next two columns.

Language Hints!

- An irregular plural noun is a noun that becomes plural by changing its spelling in other ways than adding –s or –es.

- **Example**: The plural of *loaf* is *loaves*.

Singular Noun	Plural Rule	Plural Noun
secret	*add* –s	*secrets*
key		
batch		
child		
shoe		
foot		
cookie		
glass		
lady		
lunch		

Story Elements–Character

Directions: After drinking the mixture, Andrew sits in front of his mom's full-length mirror waiting for something to happen. Draw a picture of what you think will happen to Andrew. Write two or three sentences describing your picture.

_____

_____

_____

_____

Story Elements–Plot

Directions: What do you think will happen to Andrew now that he has the freckle juice recipe? Do you think the outcome will be good or bad? In the space below, write at least three positive and three negative outcomes.

Positive Outcomes	Negative Outcomes

Vocabulary Overview

Key words and phrases from this section are provided below with definitions and sentences about how the words are used in the story. Introduce and discuss these important vocabulary words with students. If you think these words or other words in the story warrant more time devoted to them, there are suggestions in the introduction for other vocabulary activities (page 5).

Word	Definition	Sentence about Text
weak	not strong; frail	Andrew feels **weak** after drinking the freckle juice.
doorway	the passage or opening into a building or room	Mrs. Marcus stands in the **doorway** wondering what Andrew is doing.
nodded	made a slight, quick downward movement of the head	Andrew **nods**, agreeing with his mother that he is sick.
moaned	made a low sound because of physical or mental suffering	Andrew is so uncomfortable that he can't stop **moaning**.
appendicitis	inflammation of the appendix	Mrs. Marcus thinks Andrew has **appendicitis**.
ambulance	a specially equipped vehicle used to transport sick or injured people	Andrew's mom panics and wants to call for an **ambulance**.
sensible	having, using, or showing good sense or judgment	Mrs. Marcus thinks Andrew should have been more **sensible**.
tucked	fitted snugly	Andrew's mother **tucks** him into bed after giving him some pink stuff.
drifted	did something slowly, with progression	Andrew **drifts** off to sleep.
dropout	a student who withdraws before completing a course of instruction	Andrew doesn't ever want to go to school again, but his mother will not have a **dropout** in the second grade.

Name _____ Date _____

Vocabulary Activity

Directions: Complete each sentence below with one of the vocabulary words listed.

Words from the Story

weak	doorway	nod	moans	appendicitis
ambulance	sensible	tucks	drifts	dropout

1. Andrew _____ and groans after drinking the freckle juice.

2. Andrew hears his mom, but he is too _____ to answer her.

3. Mrs. Marcus stands in the _____ wondering what Andrew is doing.

4. Andrew's mom is so worried, she almost calls for an _____.

5. Andrew's mother thinks he is more _____ than to make himself something to eat.

6. Andrew's mother _____ him into bed.

Directions: Answer this question.

7. Why does Mrs. Marcus think Andrew has **appendicitis**?

_____

_____

© Shell Education

Analyzing the Literature

Provided below are discussion questions you can use in small groups, with the whole class, or for written assignments. Each question is written at two levels so that you can choose the right question for each group of students. For each question, a few key points are provided for your reference as you discuss the book with students.

Story Element	Level 1	Level 2	Key Discussion Points
Character	Why does Andrew look green?	What does Mrs. Marcus think is wrong with Andrew?	Andrew looks green because he is very sick from drinking the freckle juice. He has a horrible stomachache. Mrs. Marcus thinks Andrew has appendicitis.
Plot	What does Mrs. Marcus find when she goes into the kitchen?	Why is Mrs. Marcus so upset when she finds a mess in the kitchen?	Mrs. Marcus finds a huge mess in the kitchen. She is very upset because she told Andrew to play outside, but he didn't. He is also not allowed to cook anything by himself.
Character	How does Andrew feel about Sharon?	What do you think Andrew means when he says, "She'll be sorry some day."	Andrew says he hates her for giving him this horrible recipe. He is so upset that he is thinking about taking revenge on Sharon.
Plot	What happens in Andrew's dreams?	What is the significance of the monster getting freckles and Andrew getting none?	Andrew dreams about a big green monster making him drink freckle juice three times a day. Even though it is a dream, it shows that Andrew will never get freckles from drinking freckle juice.
Setting	Why doesn't Andrew go to school the next day?	How does Andrew's mom get him to return to school?	Andrew is still is not feeling well, plus he does not want Sharon to see him without freckles. Mrs. Marcus says Andrew will have to bathe three times a day for the next ten years if he does not go back to school.

Name _____ Date _____

Reader Response

Think

Andrew doesn't really like Sharon, yet he buys her recipe, makes it, and drinks it. Why do you think he listens to her? Would you listen to Sharon?

Opinion Writing Prompt

Why do you think Andrew buys, makes, and drinks Sharon's recipe. Make sure you give reasons to support your answer.

_____

_____

_____

_____

_____

_____

_____

_____

Guided Close Reading

Closely reread the section beginning with, "Andrew nodded." Stop reading when you reach, "His stomach was killing him."

Directions: Think about these questions. In the space below, write ideas as you think about the answers. Be ready to share your answers.

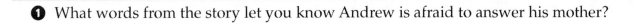

❶ What words from the story let you know Andrew is afraid to answer his mother?

❷ What text helps you understand that Andrew is in pain?

❸ Based on the events in the story, why does Andrew's mom come back to the bedroom *in a hurry?*

Name _____ Date _____

Making Connections–Make a Monster

Directions: Andrew has a dream about a monster that makes him drink freckle juice three times a day. Create your own freckle monster. Draw what your monster would look like. Then, describe your monster and whether or not it has any special characteristics and/or powers.

_____

_____

_____

_____

_____

Language Learning–Past to Present

Directions: *Freckle Juice* is written in the past tense. Read the following sentences from chapter 4. Circle all of the verbs. Once you have identified all of the verbs, rewrite the sentences in the present tense.

Language Hints!

- Most past tense verbs end in *–ed*, but some are irregular.
- Example: Andrew had drunk the freckle juice. The verb *had drunk* is in the past tense.

Past Tense	Present Tense
1. He hated Sharon.	
2. He drifted off to sleep.	
3. He had terrible dreams.	
4. A big green monster made him drink two quarts of freckle juice, three times a day.	
5. Every time he drank it, the *monster* got freckles but Andrew didn't.	

Name _____ Date _____

Story Elements-Character

Directions: Write a letter to Sharon as if you were Andrew. Tell Sharon how you feel after the freckle juice doesn't work and makes you feel sick.

Dear _____ ,

_____

_____

_____

_____

_____

_____

_____

_____

_____

From,

_____

Story Elements-Plot

Directions: Think about how Andrew feels after drinking the freckle juice. What would you do if you were in the same situation as Andrew? What would you do when you arrive at school?

_____

_____

_____

_____

_____

_____

Directions: Draw a picture of what happens when you first see Sharon.

Vocabulary Overview

Key words and phrases from this section are provided below with definitions and sentences about how the words are used in the story. Introduce and discuss these important vocabulary words with students. If you think these words or other words in the story warrant more time devoted to them, there are suggestions in the introduction for other vocabulary activities (page 5).

Word	Definition	Sentence about Text
reflection	the casting of an image; mirror like	Andrew studies his **reflection** in the car window.
decorate	to furnish or embellish	Andrew decides to **decorate** his face with the magic marker.
snapped	made a short, quick sound with the fingers	Miss Kelly **snaps** her fingers to get the children's attention.
chattering	talking rapidly	The children **chatter** about Andrew's freckle face.
formula	any fixed or conventional method for doing something	Miss Kelly offers Andrew a secret **formula** to get rid of the freckles.
removing	taking away or taking something off	Miss Kelly helps Andrew **remove** his blue freckles.
package	a bundle of something that is usually wrapped	Andrew's teacher hands him a **package** to take into the bathroom.
rub	to move back and forth against another surface	The note says to **rub** the face three times if the freckle remover doesn't work the first time.
rinse	to wash lightly by pouring water or dipping into water	Andrew must **rinse** after rubbing the remover on his face.
handsome	good looking; attractive	Miss Kelly tells Andrew he looks **handsome** without the freckles.

Name _____ Date _____

Vocabulary Activity

Directions: Practice your vocabulary and writing skills. Write at least four sentences using words from the story. Make sure your sentences show what the words mean.

Words from the Story

reflection	decorate	snap	chatter	formula
remove	package	rub	rinse	handsome

_____

_____

_____

_____

_____

_____

_____

Directions: Answer this question.

1. What is in Miss Kelly's secret **formula** for removing freckles?

_____

_____

Analyzing the Literature

Provided below are discussion questions you can use in small groups, with the whole class, or for written assignments. Each question is written at two levels so that you can choose the right question for each group of students. For each question, a few key points are provided for your reference as you discuss the book with students.

Story Element	Level 1	Level 2	Key Discussion Points
Plot	What does Andrew draw on his face?	Why does Andrew use a blue marker?	Andrew draws blue freckles on his face with a magic marker. Andrew uses a blue marker because he is in a hurry to get to school and cannot find a brown marker.
Setting	Where is Andrew when he decorates his face with blue freckles?	Why does Andrew stop two blocks before school to add the freckles to his face?	Andrew is two blocks away from school, using a car window to see his reflection as he makes freckles on his face. He does not want his mom to know, so he does not do it at home, and he cannot risk going to school without any freckles, so he finds a place in between.
Character	What does Miss Kelly give Andrew?	Why do you think Miss Kelly gives Andrew a formula for removing freckles?	Miss Kelly gives Andrew a secret formula for removing freckles. Miss Kelly understands Andrew and cares about him. She wants to give him confidence in himself without freckles.
Plot	Why does Nicky want to use the secret formula for removing freckles?	What does Sharon offer Nicky?	Nicky wants the secret formula because he hates his freckles. Sharon offers Nicky a secret recipe for removing freckles.

Name _____ Date _____

Reader Response

Think

Freckle juice didn't work the way that Andrew hoped it would. Think of a time when something you wanted didn't turn out the way you had hoped.

Narrative Writing Prompt

Write about a time when you were hoping for something to turn out a certain way but it didn't. Did it work out for the best like it did for Andrew? What did you learn from it?

_____

_____

_____

_____

_____

_____

_____

_____

Name _____ Date _____

Guided Close Reading

Closely reread the section beginning with, "I grew freckles, Miss Kelly." Stop at, ". . . the class couldn't hear."

Directions: Think about these questions. In the chart below, write ideas as you think about the answers. Be ready to share your answers.

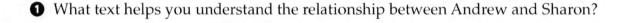

❶ What text helps you understand the relationship between Andrew and Sharon?

❷ Use the book to tell why Miss Kelly responds to the situation with, "You may sit down now, Andrew. Let's get on with our morning work."

❸ What evidence proves that Miss Kelly wasn't trying to be completely secretive about giving Andrew a formula for removing the freckles?

Making Connections–Compare and Contrast

Directions: Think about the main characters, Andrew and Sharon. In what ways are Andrew and Sharon alike? In what ways are they different? Fill in the Venn diagram with their similarities and differences.

Andrew   **Sharon**

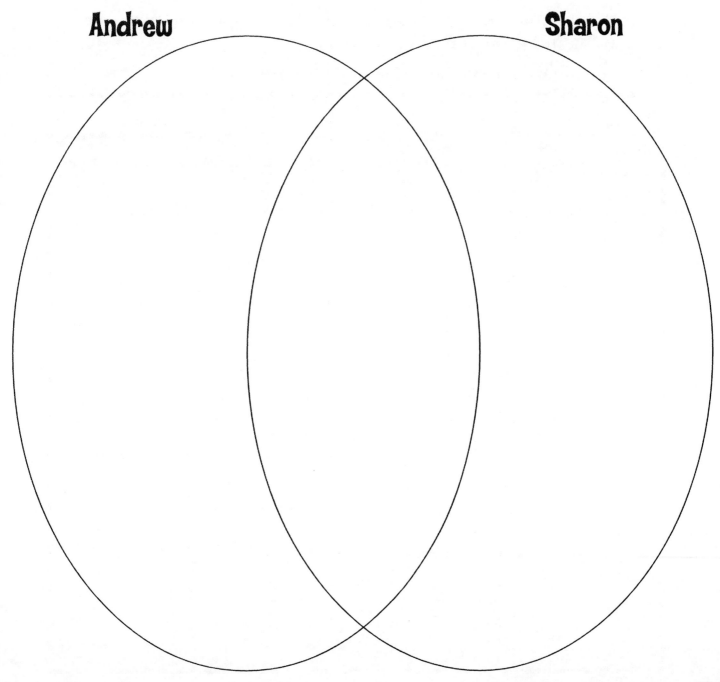

Language Learning–Name that Noun

Directions: Find eight nouns from chapter 5 and write them in the first column. Next, identify them as common or proper. Then, label each noun as a person, place, or thing.

Language Hints!

- A common noun is a word that refers to a person, place, or thing but is not a particular name.

- A proper noun is the name of a particular noun.

Noun	Common/Proper	Person/Place/Thing
breakfast	common	thing

Story Elements–Character

Directions: Think about what you know about the characters in the book. Write or draw at least five words or pictures that describe each character next to his or her name in the chart.

Andrew	
Sharon	
Mrs. Marcus	
Miss Kelly	

Name _____ Date _____

Story Elements-Plot

Directions: Think about what might happen after Sharon offers Nicky the freckle remover recipe. Add a scene to the last chapter of the book. Be sure to describe the setting and characters, and include any dialogue that may take place. Then, draw an illustration to go with the new scene.

_____

_____

_____

_____

_____

_____

Name _____ Date _____

Post-Reading Theme Thoughts

Directions: Choose a main character from the book. Pretend you are that character. Draw a picture of a happy face or a sad face to show how the character would feel about each statement. Then, use words to explain your picture.

Character I Chose: _____

Statement	How Do You Feel? 🙂 🙁	Explain Your Answer
Everyone can be trusted.		
Most people want to change something about themselves.		
Being the center of attention is fun.		
Teachers help build confidence in students.		

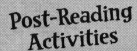

Post-Reading
Activities

Culminating Activity: We Are All Different

Andrew is not very happy with the way he looks, and he wishes he looked like his classmate, Nicky. In the end, he gains some confidence and accepts the way he looks.

Directions: We are all different, and it is important to understand those differences. In a small group, make a list of different physical characteristics on a separate sheet of paper (you might include eye color, hair color, skin color, freckles, no freckles, height).

Then, create five new characters by mixing and matching those characteristics. Draw pictures of them and write a short story about how they become friends. What problems do they encounter? Are they happy with the way they look?

1

_____

_____

Culminating Activity: We Are All Different (cont.)

2

_____

_____

3

_____

_____

Culminating Activity: We Are All Different (cont.)

4

_____

_____

5

_____

_____

Culminating Activity: We Are All Different (cont.)

Directions: Work with students to help them choose **one** of the following activities to complete using the stories they have created.

- Decide which of your newly created characters is your favorite and create a life-size figure using bulletin board paper and markers. Be prepared to describe the character's unique traits and explain why he/she is your favorite character from your story.

- Make puppets of your characters. Write a short skit, and turn your story into a puppet show.

- Rewrite your story with a different setting. Perhaps they are at the park, on the playground, or at one of their houses. Think about how this will change their interactions and dialogue.

Comprehension Assessment

Directions: Fill in the bubble for the best response to each question.

Chapter 1

1. Why does Andrew want freckles?

   (A) Nicky Lane is his best friend.

   (B) He wants to be able to count them on his own face.

   (C) He thinks they look cool.

   (D) He thinks he won't have to wash his face and neck as often.

Chapter 2

2. Why does Andrew have to wait until three o'clock to get the recipe?

   (E) Sharon forgot it and has to get it after school.

   (F) The teacher takes it away, and that's when she will return it.

   (G) Sharon says that is part of the deal.

   (H) He wants to wait until school is out to get it from Sharon.

Chapter 3

3. What does Andrew **not** do while drinking the freckle juice?

   (A) holds his nose

   (B) spills it

   (C) tilts his head back

   (D) gulps it down

Comprehension Assessment *(cont.)*

Chapter 4

4. In what ways does Andrew disappoint his mother?

_____

_____

_____

_____

_____

_____

Chapter 5

5. What characteristic does **not** describe Andrew?

(E) jealous

(F) impatient

(G) patient

(H) determined

Name _____ Date _____

Response to Literature:
We All Make Mistakes

Directions: Andrew makes some mistakes, or perhaps bad decisions, that are not carefully thought out. Choose a scene from the book where you think Andrew makes a mistake or a bad decision. Draw a picture of it and answer the questions on page 69 about that scene. Use color and be neat!

Response to Literature:
We All Make Mistakes (cont.)

1. What is happening in this scene, and what is Andrew's bad decision?

_____

_____

_____

2. How does this affect the rest of the book?

_____

_____

_____

3. What should Andrew have done instead?

_____

_____

_____

4. How would this better decision affect the rest of the book?

_____

_____

_____

Name _____ Date _____

Response to Literature Rubric

Directions: Use this rubric to evaluate student responses.

Great Job	Good Work	Keep Trying
☐ You answered all four questions completely. You included many details.	☐ You answered all four questions.	☐ You did not answer all four questions.
☐ Your handwriting is very neat. There are no spelling errors.	☐ Your handwriting can be neater. There are some spelling errors.	☐ Your handwriting is not very neat. There are many spelling errors.
☐ Your picture is neat and fully colored.	☐ Your picture is neat and some of it is colored.	☐ Your picture is not very neat and/or fully colored.
☐ Creativity is clear in both the picture and the writing.	☐ Creativity is clear in either the picture or the writing.	☐ There is not much creativity in either the picture or the writing.

Teacher Comments: _____

_____

_____

_____

The responses provided here are just examples of what students may answer. Many accurate responses are possible for the questions throughout this unit.

Vocabulary Activity—Section 1:
Chapter 1 (page 15)

1. Sharon wants to sell Andrew a freckle juice **recipe**.

Guided Close Reading—Section 1:
Chapter 1 (page 18)

1. Based on the tone of his responses, Nicky seems to be annoyed. He says things like, "What do you mean *how?* You get *born* with them. That's how!"
2. Andrew finally gets to be line leader, but it's "some luck" that Sharon is the girls' line leader at the same time.
3. Andrew is annoyed with Sharon because he thinks she is a know-it-all. His tone when he asks her, "Who asked *you?*" proves his annoyance.

Making Connections—Section 1:
Chapter 1 (page 19)

Some examples of math problems may include:

500,000 + 500,000 = 1,000,000

4,000,000 − 3,000,000 = 1,000,000

1,000,000 x 1= 1,000,000

4,000,000 ÷ 4 = 1,000,000

Language Learning—Section 1:
Chapter 1 (page 20)

1. **Incorrect**—Miss Kelly called, "Andrew, are you paying attention?"
2. **Incorrect**—"What do you want?" Nicky asked.
3. **Correct**
4. **Correct**
5. **Incorrect**—Sharon said, "I've got six on my nose."

Vocabulary Activity—Section 2:
Chapter 2 (page 25)

- Mrs. Marcus almost trips on her long **bathrobe**.
- It is five weeks of Andrew's **allowance**.
- He **wraps** them in a tissue and stuffs them in his pocket.
- Andrew turns the **combination** of his safe-bank to the right numbers.
- The recipe lands in the middle of the **aisle**.
1. The freckle juice recipe lands in the middle of the **aisle**, and when Andrew tries to get it, he falls over.

Guided Close Reading—Section 2:
Chapter 2 (page 28)

1. Sharon antagonizes Andrew by responding with, "Bring what?" as her eyes open real wide. She also says she has it as she pats her pocket, not letting him see it.
2. Andrew tries to tease her back by saying he has the money, as he pats *his* pocket, just as she did.
3. No, Sharon does not give in. She says, "Sorry Andrew. A deal's a deal!" She waits for the money first.

Making Connections—Section 2:
Chapter 2 (page 30)

Answers will vary, but they may include:

- 1 dime, 8 nickels
- 2 dimes, 6 nickels
- 3 dimes, 4 nickels
- 4 dimes, 2 nickels
- 1 quarter, 5 nickels
- 1 quarter, 1 dime, 3 nickels
- 1 quarter, 2 dimes, 1 nickel

Language Learning—Section 2:
Chapter 2 (page 31)

Answers will vary but may include:

Andrew: determined, clumsy, focused
Sharon: sly, witty, mean, dishonest
Miss Kelly: patient, observant, smart

Vocabulary Activity—Section 3:
Chapter 3 (page 35)

1. Andrew's foot might get too **sweaty**, so he doesn't put the recipe inside his sock.
2. Andrew's mother is **dealing** cards when he gets there.
3. Andrew **dashes** home to read the recipe.
4. Andrew gets an onion from the **basement**.
5. Andrew **gulps** down the awful tasting freckle juice.

Guided Close Reading—Section 3:
Chapter 3 (page 38)

1. Andrew thinks carefully because he realizes that inside his sock might be too sweaty and might cause the ink to blur. He also mentions that it would be safe from the wind in his shoe.
2. He mentions he is a slow reader and he does not want to waste any time getting home.
3. The first two sentences prove he forgets. They say Andrew runs all the way home and *then* he remembers he has to go to Mrs. Burrow's house to get the key.

Answer Key

Language Learning—Section 3:
Chapter 3 (page 40)

secret	add –s	secrets
key	add –s	keys
batch	add –es	batches
child	irregular	children
shoe	add –s	shoes
foot	irregular	feet
cookie	add –s	cookies
glass	add –es	glasses
lady	change y to i and add –es	ladies
lunch	add –es	lunches

Vocabulary Activity—Section 4:
Chapter 4 (page 44)

1. Andrew **moans** and groans after drinking the freckle juice.
2. Andrew hears his mom, but he is too **weak** to answer her.
3. Mrs. Marcus stands in the **doorway** wondering what Andrew is doing.
4. Andrew's mom is so worried, she almost calls for an **ambulance**.
5. Andrew's mother thinks he is more **sensible** than to make himself something to eat.
6. Andrew's mother **tucks** him into bed.
7. Mrs. Marcus thinks Andrew has **appendicitis** because he is having such bad stomach pain.

Guided Close Reading—Section 4:
Chapter 4 (page 47)

1. Andrew is afraid to open his mouth and answer his mother because he thinks he will lose the freckle juice.
2. Andrew is clearly in pain because he moans and holds his stomach.
3. Andrew's mom comes back to the bedroom in a hurry because she is so upset at the mess she finds when she enters the kitchen.

Language Learning—Section 4:
Chapter 4 (page 49)

1. He **hates** Sharon.
2. He **drifts** off to sleep.
3. He **has** terrible dreams.
4. A big green monster **makes** him drink two quarts of freckle juice, three times a day.
5. Every time he **drinks** it, the monster **gets** freckles but Andrew **doesn't**.

Vocabulary Activity—Section 5:
Chapter 5 (page 53)

1. Miss Kelly's secret formula is probably soap, water, and lemon juice since Andrew mentions it smelling like lemons.

Guided Close Reading—Section 5:
Chapter 5 (page 56)

1. The text that describes Andrew and Sharon's relationship in this section is: "He turned toward Sharon and stuck out his tongue. Sharon made a frog face at him." This shows they annoy each other and often provoke one another.
2. Miss Kelly chooses to downplay the situation with her comment. She does not want to get involved quite yet; she wants Andrew to think about his decision to have blue freckles before she offers a solution.
3. The text that proves she's not being too secretive is: "Her voice was low, but not so low that the class couldn't hear."

Making Connections—Section 5
Chapter 5 (page 57)

Answers will vary but may include:

Andrew: believing, clumsy

Both: immature, annoying to each other

Sharon: smart, sly, witty

Language Learning—Section 5:
Chapter 5 (page 58)

Students will find various examples, but some may include:

- Andrew, proper, person
- stomach, common, thing
- bedroom, common, thing
- Magic Marker, proper, thing

Comprehension Assessment (pages 66–67)

1. D. He thinks he won't have to wash his face and neck as often.
2. F. The teacher takes it away, and that's when she will return it.
3. B. spills it
4. Andrew disappoints his mother because he doesn't change his clothes, he makes a mess in the kitchen, and he doesn't play outside like his mother asked him to do.
5. G. patient